THE USBORNE
FIRST BOOK
OF
MUSIC

Emma Danes

Illustrated by Norman Young
Designed by Carol Law
Edited by Anthony Marks

Music education consultant: Christine Richards

Contents

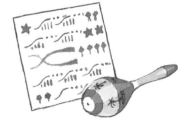

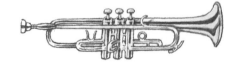

Introduction

Throughout history, people all around the world have been singing and playing musical instruments, dancing and making up new music. For many people, music is a hobby and entertainment, which they enjoy both with their friends and by themselves. Music can also be a serious way of showing other people what you think and feel, just like writing or painting.

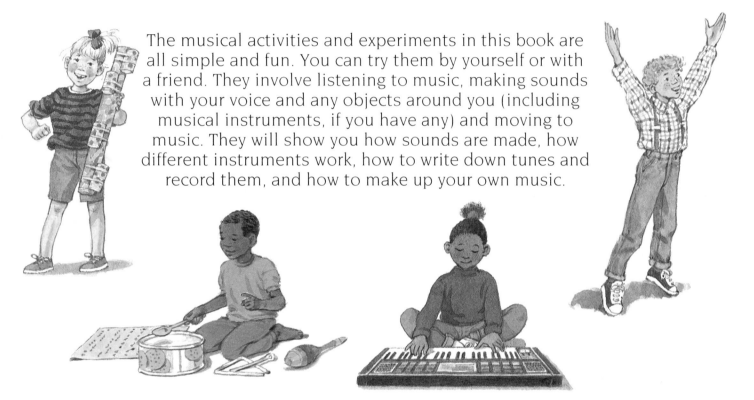

The musical activities and experiments in this book are all simple and fun. You can try them by yourself or with a friend. They involve listening to music, making sounds with your voice and any objects around you (including musical instruments, if you have any) and moving to music. They will show you how sounds are made, how different instruments work, how to write down tunes and record them, and how to make up your own music.

Later in the book, you can read about the jobs musicians do, the music people play in different parts of the world, and what music was like in the past. You can also find out how most music today is written down, and how to read it. There is also advice about choosing an instrument to learn, and lots of suggestions for music to listen to.

What is music?

Music is made up of sounds which are arranged in patterns. The sounds can be ones you make with your voice, with musical instruments or with any other objects. You can make the sounds long or short, high or low, and loud or quiet. No two pieces of music sound exactly the same.

High and low sounds

Sounds can be high or low, or in between. The highness or lowness of a sound is called its pitch. Tunes are patterns of sounds of different pitch.

Sing a tune and listen carefully to how the sounds go up and down. Then follow this wavy line with a finger, singing. As the line goes down, sing lower. As it goes up, sing higher.

A whistle has a high sound.

A bass drum has a low sound.

Draw the outline of buildings, trees or hills you can see from a window. Then sing as you follow the line to invent a tune.

Now try drawing a wavy line as you sing a tune, going up where the tune goes up, and down where it goes down.

Hundreds of years ago, people drew curved lines above the words of songs to remind them where the tune went up or down.

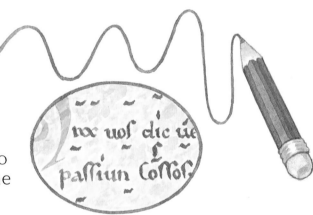

Long and short sounds

As well as a pattern of pitches, most music has patterns of long and short sounds, and silences too. These patterns are called rhythms.

Listen to rhythms around you. Some are made up of sounds which are all the same length. Others have long and short sounds, in a regular pattern, or jumbled together.

Horse trotting

Clock ticking

Your heart beating

Cat purring

Telephone ringing

Bird singing

4

Read out the words below, clapping the rhythm you make.

Say	each	word	and	clap	your	hands.
CLAP	CLAP	CLAP	CLAP	CLAP	CLAP	CLAP

Long	sounds and	short - er	sounds
CLAP	CLAP - CLAP	CLAP - CLAP	CLAP

This is the simplest rhythm of all. Each sound is the same length.

This rhythm has a long sound, then four shorter sounds then a long sound.

Loud and quiet sounds

Music can be loud or quiet. It can also change, slowly or suddenly, from one to the other. The loudness or quietness of a sound is called its volume.

Hold one hand flat. Tap it with one finger. It makes a quiet sound. Next tap with two fingers, then three, then four. The sound gets louder.

Make a sound like a siren. Start quietly and get louder, then quieter again, as though the siren gets closer, passes you, then goes away.

Different sounds

Music is full of different kinds of sounds. You can make many sounds with your voice and objects around you. Try the ideas below, listening to how different each sound is.

Gently tap a spoon on different objects. You could try a cup, a saucepan, a table and a refrigerator. How many sounds can you make?

Close your eyes, and listen to some friends talking. Guess who is speaking from the sound of each voice.

Use a cassette player to record your friends saying "Hello, how are you?". Then play the tape back. Can you tell which voice is which?

5

Making sounds

All sounds, whether they are noises like crashes and bangs, or tunes played on a musical instrument, happen because something shivers very quickly from side to side. There are only a few ways to make something shiver like this, so you play all musical instruments in similar ways.

Some you bang, shake or scrape.

Some you blow.

Others you pluck or play with a bow.

How sounds happen

The way things shiver when they make a sound is called vibration. Try these experiments to see how instruments vibrate and make sounds.

Wrap some stiff tissue paper around a comb. Hum on the paper and feel your lips tingle as it shivers. This is how a kazoo works.

Kazoo

Recorder

Tape some paper tightly over one end of a cardboard tube. Sing into the tube, gently touching the paper. It vibrates, because your voice vibrates the air in the tube. To play a recorder, you blow it so the air in it vibrates.

Tap an empty metal tin with a spoon. Feel it vibrate as it makes a sound. This is like playing a triangle.

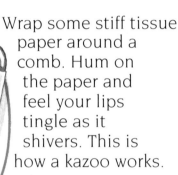

Triangle

Your voice makes sounds when part of your throat vibrates. You may feel this if you touch your throat as you speak or sing.

Stretch a rubber band and pluck it. See and feel it vibrate. If you pluck harder, it vibrates harder and sounds louder. This is like plucking guitar strings.

Guitar

How you hear sounds

If you drop a pebble into water, ripples spread out from it. Bigger pebbles make bigger ripples. The ripples are the water vibrating.

The ripples die out further away and then stop. This is because the water vibrations die out.

When things vibrate they make the air around them vibrate too. Air vibrations spread out from vibrating objects like ripples. When the air vibrations reach you, a thin skin inside your ear vibrates. Then you hear a sound. You hear different sounds because each instrument makes the air vibrate differently in your ear.

Big vibrations sound loud.

Small vibrations sound quiet.

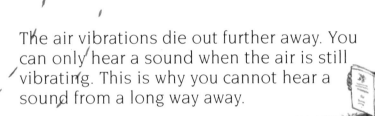

The air vibrations die out further away. You can only hear a sound when the air is still vibrating. This is why you cannot hear a sound from a long way away.

Sound boxes

Many instruments have hollow parts called sound boxes. When you play them, the air in the sound box vibrates, making the sound louder.

Violin strings are stretched over a wooden sound box.

A drum is a large hollow sound box.

The box part of a xylophone is a sound box.

Sound box

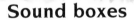

7

Making high and low sounds

The highness or lowness of a sound is called its pitch. When you sing a tune, you sing a pattern of notes of different pitches. Sounds are made when things vibrate, or shiver very quickly. (For more about this, see pages 6-7.) The pitch of a note depends on how fast or slow the vibrations are. The experiments on these pages show how musical instruments make different notes.

Fast and slow vibrations

Fast vibrations make higher pitches than slow vibrations. Our ears can hear pitches made by vibrations as slow as 20 a second and as fast as 20,000 a second. Some insects vibrate their wings to fly. You hear the vibrations as a buzz. The faster the vibrations, the higher the buzz.

A mosquito's wings move fast and make a high buzz.

A fly's wings move more slowly. Their buzz is lower than a mosquito's.

Bees' wings are even slower so make a lower buzz.

Butterflies move their wings so slowly that we cannot hear the sound they make.

Tapping tunes

Tap an empty glass jar near the top with a pen or pencil. Sing the note it makes.

Pour water slowly into the jar. Keep tapping and listen to how the note changes.

You make the jar and water vibrate when you tap. The pitch gets lower when you add more water, because the jar vibrates more slowly.

You can tap tunes using several jars with different amounts of water in.

Xylophone bars are different lengths. Shorter bars vibrate faster than longer bars when you tap them.

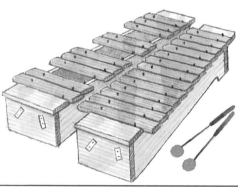

The long bars make low notes.

The short bars make high notes.

Blowing tunes

Blow over the top of an empty bottle until you make a note. Pour some water into the bottle and blow again. Notice how the note gets higher as you add more water.

This time, you make the air in the bottle vibrate, not the bottle and water. Adding water pushes some air out. The air left vibrates faster and makes a higher pitch.

Panpipes have long and short pipes. The long pipes have more air in, so they make lower notes.

Plucking tunes

Stretch an elastic band over an open, empty box. Pluck the elastic band and sing the note it makes.

Try thicker or thinner bands that are the same length. Try shorter and longer bands. You have to stretch short ones more tightly. Thin, tight bands vibrate faster than thick, loose ones, so make higher pitches.

Most guitars have six strings. Some strings are thinner and tighter than others.

Pegs to tighten and loosen the strings

The thicker, looser strings make low notes.

The thinner, tighter strings make higher notes.

Now tie a piece of strong, thin string to a door handle. (The door has to be shut.)

Stretch out a little string, pull it as tight as you can and pluck it.

Try stretching out a lot more string, pulling as tight as you can and plucking. The note changes.

Long strings vibrate more slowly than short strings, so they make lower pitches.

A harp has many strings of different lengths.

The short strings make high notes.

The longer strings make lower notes.

Instruments you bang, shake or scrape

Instruments that you bang, shake or scrape are called percussion instruments. There are many different kinds. Most are for making rhythms (patterns of long and short sounds).

Claves are wooden sticks that you bang together.

Castanets have two pieces of wood on a cord. You wind the cord around a thumb and finger, and click the wood parts together. Spanish flamenco dancers often click castanets.

Castanets

Claves

Maracas

A guiro has ridges which you scrape to make a sound.

Guiro

Maracas have a hollow case filled with things which rattle as you shake.

A glockenspiel has metal bars. It sounds different from a xylophone which has wooden bars. You play it with hard sticks.

Glockenspiel

Different kinds of drums

Drums are played all over the world. You hit or tap them with your hands or with sticks.

Bongos are small drums from South America. You tap them with your fingers and hands.

Bongos

Steel pans

African talking drums have strings which you squeeze. This tightens the skin so you make higher sounds. Talking drums can sound like voices. Good players can tap messages on them.

Talking drum

Kettledrums also play different notes. You tighten the skin with metal screws to make higher notes.

Steel pans are from the West Indies. To make different notes you hit the tops in different places.

Screw

Kettledrum

10

A drum kit has cymbals and several kinds of drums in it.

Cymbal

Hi-hat cymbals

Snare drum

Cymbal

Tom toms

Floor tom

Bass drum

Pedal

Snare drums have wires just under the skin which make a loud rattle.

You press a pedal on the bass drum to make the drumstick hit the skin.

Tom toms are smaller than floor toms. They make higher sounds.

Cymbals are metal discs that make a crash when you hit them.

You use drumsticks or wire brushes to play the instruments in a drum kit.

Pianos

A piano is a percussion instrument, because when you press the keys, hammers hit the strings inside.

You can see this happen if you look inside a piano. Ask an adult to lift up the lid.

As you let go of a key, a block of wood covered with felt, called a damper, stops the string from vibrating.

Side view of hammer, damper and string

Hammer

Damper

String

Percussion instruments to make

To make some maracas, find two empty yogurt cartons the same size. Put a handful of rice or beads in one carton. Tape the other carton upside down on top of it.

Try sand, pebbles, macaroni and other fillings to make different sounds.

Try pushing rice, paper clips or macaroni into a balloon. Then blow it up and shake it.

You can make a giant shaker with one long cardboard tube and several short ones.

Put rice or beads in the short tubes. Tape paper over the ends and attach them to the long tube with rubber bands. You could decorate or paint the tubes.

Try out lots of ways to play your giant shaker. You can shake it, tap it, bang it on the floor, or drag it along railings. The long tube is a sound box (see page 7), which makes the sound louder.

Instruments you blow

Instruments that you blow are known as wind instruments. They make a sound when you blow because you make the air inside them vibrate. The more air there is vibrating, the lower the note sounds. You blow wind instruments in different ways.

Ways to blow

You can blow over a mouthpiece to make the air in the instrument vibrate.

You can blow onto strips of cane, which vibrate and make the air inside vibrate.

You can buzz your lips in a special mouthpiece to make the air inside vibrate.

Flute

Strips of cane called reeds

Saxophone

Bassoon

Tuba

Playing different notes

You play different notes on a wind instrument by covering up holes or changing the length of tube. This changes the amount of air vibrating.

Recorders have finger holes. When they are all uncovered, the air in the tube is blown out through all of them.

If you cover some holes with your fingers as you blow, you trap more air in the tube. This makes lower notes.

Oboes have keys and levers. You press these to cover the holes you cannot reach with your fingers.

Oboe

Trumpets have keys called valves. When they are pressed they open extra parts of the tube to make different notes. Trumpeters also make other notes by changing the shape of their lips.

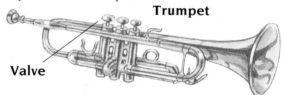

Trumpet

Valve

Trombones have a sliding part. You move this to make the tube longer or shorter, so you play different notes.

Trombone

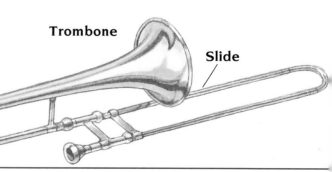

Slide

Instruments with air pumps

Other instruments have air pumps to push air through them and make sounds.

Bagpipes

Bagpipers blow air into a bag and then squeeze it out through pipes. The sounds happen as the air goes through the pipes. One pipe has finger holes so you can change the note.

An organ has a keyboard like a piano, but it is a wind instrument. The keys are linked to huge pipes. When you press a key, air is pumped through one of the pipes. The pipes are different lengths, so they play different notes.

There are several pipes for each note, each with a different sound.

Organ

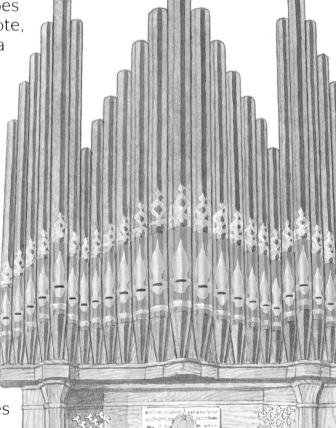

You pull knobs called stops to choose which pipes to use.

Stops ——

You play extra notes using foot pedals.

Foot pedals —

Wind instruments to make

To make a straw oboe, cut the top of a drinking straw into a point and pinch it to make it flatter. This part is like a reed.

Fold your lips over your teeth, put the straw in your mouth and blow hard. Keep trying until you make a squawk. You will feel the reed vibrate.

If you snip the straw as you blow, less air can vibrate inside. The note gets higher.

Try cutting finger holes. Cover and uncover them to change the note.

To cut holes, pinch straw.

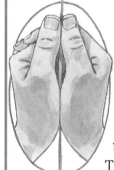

Stretch a blade of grass tightly between your thumbs. Try to make a sound by blowing on it. The blade of grass is like a reed.

Instruments with strings

To make strings vibrate, you can pluck them or use a special stick with hair attached to it, called a bow. To use a bow, you stroke the string with the hair to make it vibrate gently. The shorter and tighter the string is, the higher the note it makes when it vibrates.

Using your fingers to play different notes

Strings of different lengths make different notes. One way to shorten a string is to press it with a finger.

Stretch a rubber band around a tin lid. Pluck the band gently inside the lid, so it vibrates without slapping against the tin. All of the band inside the lid vibrates.

Now press the rubber band onto the lid with a finger and pluck it. Your finger stops some of it from vibrating.

This part does not vibrate.

The part vibrating is shorter, so you make a higher note.

You play different notes on a guitar by pressing the strings down with the fingers of your left hand. Little bars called frets under the strings show you where to press.

Plectrum

You pluck with your right hand fingers and thumb, or a piece of plastic called a plectrum.

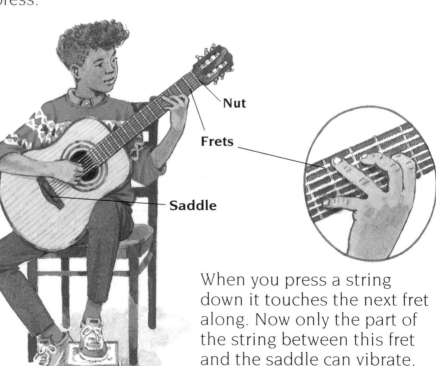

Nut

Frets

Saddle

The strings are held by a holder called the saddle at the bottom, and a bar called the nut at the top. If you pluck a string without pressing it, it vibrates from top to bottom.

When you press a string down it touches the next fret along. Now only the part of the string between this fret and the saddle can vibrate, so you make a higher note.

14

Using a bow

Many stringed instruments are usually played with a bow. You move the bow across the strings to make them vibrate.

A cello is like a large violin. You hold it between your legs to play.

The part of the bow which touches the strings is made of horsehair. You rub a sticky stuff called rosin onto the hair. This helps the hair to grip the strings as you play. You also tighten the hair with a screw so that it grips better.

Sometimes you tap the strings with the wooden part of the bow to make a different noise.

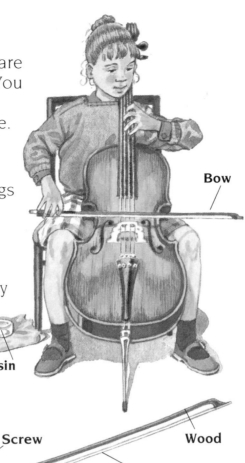

Bow

Rosin

Screw

Wood

Horsehair

Keyboards with plucked strings

Harpsichords have strings inside which are plucked by things called quills. As you press a key, a part called a jack moves up, and the quill on it plucks the string. As you let go of the key, the jack moves down and a piece of felt stops the string from vibrating.

The harpsichord was invented many years before the piano. It usually has two keyboards instead of one. These can be used to make different sounds.

A stringed instrument to make

Find a cardboard box or carton, such as a large fruit juice carton. Cover up any holes with tape. This part is the sound box.

Ask an adult to make a 3cm (1in) slit at one end, and cut a hole next to it.

Slit

Copy the shape below onto strong cardboard and cut it out.

4cm (1½in)

1cm (½in)

1cm (½in)

3cm (1in)

Push the 3cm (1in) edge into the slit in your box.

Stretch four different sized rubber bands over the box and pluck them. Press the bands down to make different notes.

Electric and electronic instruments

Without electricity, electric instruments make very quiet sounds, and electronic instruments make no sound at all. The electricity sends the vibrations made by an electric or electronic instrument through a loudspeaker. The loudspeaker vibrates as well, making the sounds loud enough to hear.

Electric guitars

Electric guitars are used mainly in pop and rock music. They can play very loudly, and make many different sounds.

Most modern electric guitars do not have a sound box. Instead the string vibrations are picked up by special microphones called pick-ups.

Pick-ups

The pick-ups change the vibrations into electrical signals. These signals are then fed into a machine called an amplifier.

Amplifier

The amplifier converts the signals back into sounds by sending them through the loudspeaker.

Loudspeaker

Bass guitar

Electric bass guitars play lower notes than other guitars. Most of them have four strings instead of six.

You can change the sound an electric guitar makes by plugging boxes called effects units into your amplifier. Each box changes the sound in a certain way when you press a pedal, for example, by making it echo or go fuzzy.

You can also plug an electronic drum machine into an amplifier. Drum machines can make lots of rhythms. Often you can store and play back rhythms you have made up yourself as well.

Effects unit

Drum machine

Other electric instruments

Some instruments, such as violins, can be made into electric instruments by adding pick-ups. This makes them louder and means they can make different sounds.

Electric violin

16

Electronic keyboards

The most popular modern electronic instruments are keyboards. Some of them are small enough for you to carry around. Others are very large. Almost all of them store sounds digitally (as patterns of numbers or digits).

In electronic keyboards, the part that vibrates to make the sound is called the oscillator. The sounds then go through an amplifier and come out of a loudspeaker.

Most modern machines store the patterns of numbers that make the sounds in a tiny part called a microprocessor.

Keyboards can imitate the sounds of many other instruments, or even a whole band. You choose which sounds you want to play by pressing a button.

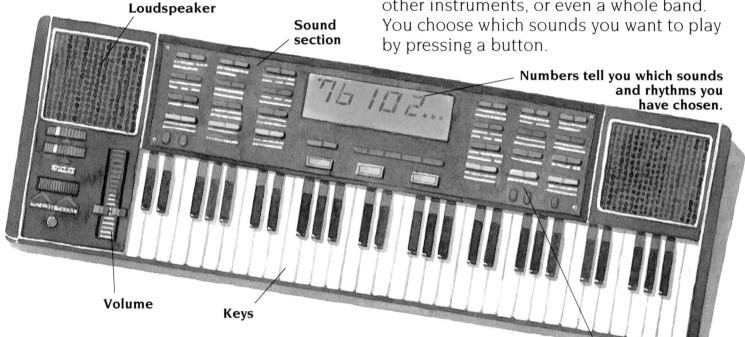

Loudspeaker

Sound section

Numbers tell you which sounds and rhythms you have chosen.

Volume

Keys

Rhythm section

Most keyboards have built-in drum rhythms. You press a button to choose which rhythm to hear, and then play along to it.

Some keyboards can add groups of notes called chords to your tune as you play. They can sometimes store your tunes too, so that you can play them back later.

You can use a special system called MIDI to connect most keyboards to a computer. This means you can play a huge range of different sounds and store them in the computer's memory.

Inventing sounds

Some keyboards let you invent sounds by changing the patterns of digits.

They also let you digitally record any sound, such as a dog barking. Then you can change the sound, for example by altering its pitch and length.

17

Using your voice

Your voice is a musical instrument which can make lots of
sounds. It works by making air vibrate as you breathe in and out.

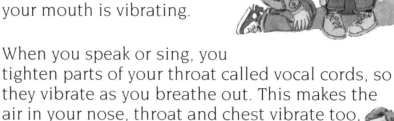

Think about sounds you can make by changing the shape of
your mouth as you breathe out. For example, try saying
"shhhh" and "ssss". Try whistling and whispering too. These
sounds are all quiet
because only the air inside
your mouth is vibrating.

When you speak or sing, you
tighten parts of your throat called vocal cords, so
they vibrate as you breathe out. This makes the
air in your nose, throat and chest vibrate too,
so you make a louder sound.

Like strings, vocal cords make higher notes the tighter and shorter
they are. You tighten and loosen your vocal cords to sing high and
low notes. Men usually have lower voices than women and
children because their vocal cords are longer.

You use your vocal cords without thinking to speak or
sing. Even babies use them automatically, when they cry.

Making all sorts of sounds

You can use your voice to make lots of
different sound effects.

Try saying the word "what" in different ways.
Say it as though you were angry, or bored, or
frightened, or asking a question. See how
many sounds you can make with it.

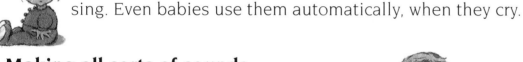

Imagine a funny machine. It might turn
straws into crayons, or balloons into hats.
Think of the sounds it might make, and
say or sing them. Try things like:

Ping pong pang
Bim bam whooosh
Ticka tacka tick tack
Click clack cloo

Making up sounds or nonsense words
while you sing is called scat singing.

How to sing better

Stand up straight and hold your head up. This helps the air to get in and out easily. Relax and do not hunch your shoulders. Imagine you are singing to people who are a long way away.

Breathe deeply, so you can sing for longer before you need to take another breath.

Open your mouth wide to make the sound louder. Sing any words very clearly.

Sing as high and low as you can to exercise the muscles around your vocal cords.

Try singing the words of different exciting, sad or funny stories, making the sound of your voice fit with the mood of the words.

Some singing games

Try singing the first two notes of a well known song, without the words, to your friends. Can they guess what it is? If not, sing the first three notes, then four notes, then five notes, and so on, until they can. How many notes do you have to sing before they can guess what the tune is?

Try to remember tunes that you hear. Ask a friend to sing four notes in a made up tune. Try to sing the same four notes back. Then try with five notes and six notes, and so on. How many notes can you remember at a time? Can you improve your score?

Singing in groups

A group of singers is often called a choir. Choirs can be very small, with only about 12 people, or huge, with about 200 people.

Sometimes an orchestra (lots of people playing instruments) joins a choir.

Operas and musicals are plays set to music. The actors sing most of the words. Sometimes they dance too.

19

How music works

Lots of things have happened to a piece of music before you hear it. First it had to be invented and may have been written down. Then someone had to play it, and someone else may have recorded the playing. When you have heard it, you might also dance to it, or use it as part of some of the music games in this book.

Inventing music and writing it down

Inventing music is called composing. You can think up music in your head or invent it by trying out sounds on an instrument. In your music, you can try to describe thoughts and feelings, or imitate sounds such as rain falling or birds singing. When you turn the page you will find some ideas for composing your own music.

To help you remember some music you have made up, you can invent signs for each kind of sound and write them down. For other people to play your music, you have to write it down in a special way so they can understand it. You can find out more about the most common way to write music down, and how to read it, later in the book.

Playing music

Once music is written down, other people can sing or play it. There is no one right way to sing or play a piece of music. Each person will have their own special way, called their interpretation. Each interpretation will make the same music sound slightly different.

You do not have to play a piece of music on the instruments for which the composer wrote it. Sometimes we do not know what a composer writing a long time ago wanted anyway. Lots of famous music has been arranged (rewritten) for other instruments, or to make it easier to play.

20

Recording music

If you record music, many more people can hear it. As you make a recording, you can change the way the sounds of different singers or instruments blend together. You can also record extra sounds and effects to add in. You can find out more about ways of recording sounds and music later in the book.

Equipment to record music was only invented about 150 years ago. To find out how music sounded before that, we have to study old books and instruments. Sometimes we can only guess how a piece sounded when it was first played hundreds of years ago.

Early recording equipment

Listening to music

The people who listen to music are very important too. The money they spend on going to concerts and buying recordings enables the musicians to do more concerts and recordings.

People called critics write in newspapers and magazines about concerts and recordings they have heard. Their articles are called reviews. People read them for advice about which musicians and pieces of music to listen to.

You could keep a notebook and write your own reviews of the music you hear.

Dancing to music

Dancers, like musicians, interpret music. Each dancer will interpret a piece of music differently to show their own thoughts and feelings.

Musical shapes

Every piece of music needs a shape. Like a story, it has to have a beginning, a middle and an end. The shape helps the music make sense, so that people can enjoy listening to it.

Beginnings and endings

A piece of music has to be interesting at the start, to make you want to listen to the rest of it. It also needs a good ending so that you remember it afterwards.

Listen to a song or piece you like. What is it at the start that makes you carry on listening? Is there a good tune, an interesting rhythm, or exciting or mysterious sounds?

Does the music end loudly or fade away? Some pieces have a special section of music at the end, called a coda, to help finish them off. Coda means tail in Italian.

Repeating patterns

Music often has repeating tune or rhythm patterns, to give it a shape. A pattern that repeats over and over again is called an ostinato. Ostinato is the Italian for obstinate, which means stubborn. Try saying the stubborn phrases on the right:

I want to, I want to, I want to!

No I won't, no I won't, no I won't!

Please can I go, please can I go, please can I go, please can I go?

Clap once as you say each word. The patterns you make are ostinato rhythms.

tap	clap	rub
tap	clap	rub
tap	clap	rub

Make three different sounds with your hands. You could tap them on your knees, clap, and rub them together. Repeat the pattern a few times listening to the sound.

Try making an ostinato pattern of three sounds with your voice. You could sing each sound to a different note.

oo ah ee oo ah ee oo ah ee oo ah ee

tip tap top tip tap top tip tap top

With a friend, make a piece of music by repeating different patterns one after the other, then together. Before you start, decide how many times to repeat each pattern, and how to end the piece.

Back to front patterns

You can make the patterns more interesting by repeating them back to front.

Make three different sounds, or sing three notes. Then make them back to front

Mix up back to front patterns with repeating patterns. Try this with a friend. Add in surprises, such as getting faster or louder.

> tip top tap tap top tip
>
> oo ah ee ee ah oo

Sandwich music

Lots of music is sandwich shaped, with the same at the beginning and end (the bread) and something else in between (the filling).

Try making musical sandwiches with a friend. One of you can be the bread, the other one the filling. Try these ideas, then make up your own.

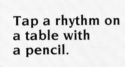

Tap a rhythm on a table with a pencil.

Then click your fingers steadily and evenly.

Then repeat the pencil tapping.

Sing some words to a made up tune four times.

Then sing different words to a new tune four times.

Repeat the first tune four times.

Use an instrument to make some long, lazy sounds.

Then make short, spiky sounds.

Finish with the long, lazy sounds you began with.

This sandwich shape is sometimes called ternary form.

Other pieces of music are like a double decker sandwich. They have two layers of filling. The two filling layers can be the same as each other, or they can be different.

> **Bread cheese bread cheese bread**
>
> **Bread cheese bread sausage bread**

Use one sound pattern for bread, another for cheese and another for sausage to make your musical double decker sandwich.

This double decker shape is often called rondo form.

Musical ideas

You can make up your own pieces of music by trying out sounds and fitting them together, or by using sounds to tell a story or describe something. You can do this by yourself or with a friend.

Trying out sounds

Try out lots of sounds using instruments, other objects and your voice. Try making sounds as high and low, loud and quiet, fast and slow as you can. Arrange them in patterns to make musical pieces.

See how many sounds you can make on an instrument. For example you can shake, tap, bang or scratch a tambourine.

Say your name over and over again, clapping the rhythm of the words. Try getting louder or quieter, or playing the rhythm on an instrument.

With some friends, try fitting your different name patterns together.

Try making lots of different drum sounds using boxes, tins and other objects for drums, and spoons and pencils as drumsticks.

Music for a rainy day

Try making up some music to describe a rainy, stormy day.

Think of pattering sounds for the first raindrops. Make the sounds louder and faster for heavier rain.

Think of rumbling, crashing sounds for thunder. They could be quiet at first, then louder.

You could pluck a stringed instrument or drum your fingertips on a table.

Try crashing cymbals, banging a drum or shaking a large sheet of thin cardboard.

You could end the piece with quiet pattering sounds again.

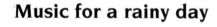

24

Music for a walk in the jungle

Make up a piece of music about a walk in the jungle. Think up sounds to describe the different animals you see.

You might choose bold, fierce sounds for tigers, slithery sounds for snakes, jumpy sounds for monkeys, and fluttery sounds for butterflies.

In between, you could have walking music, and sounds like swishing grass.

Music for a fair

Think of sounds to describe different fair rides.

For the rollercoaster you could have sounds going up and down.

For the merry-go-round you could keep repeating a pattern, like something going around in circles.

For a ghost train you could have weird, ghostly sounds mixed with train sounds.

Try making the sounds for each ride first, then putting them all together at the end.

Music for a story

Choose a story, or make one up, and invent a piece of music to go with it.

Think of sounds that go with each character. You could have lively, gentle, scary, spiky or sad sounds for different people.

Make up music for each new scene in the story. You could use lots of exciting sounds for a spooky house, magic forests, or a trip in outer space.

Then ask a friend to read the story aloud. Add in all the music and sounds you have planned.

25

Drawing and painting music

If you want to remember some music you have heard or made up, you can draw shapes to remind you of the sounds. Your shapes can show how high or low, loud or quiet, long or short the sounds are. You can also invent new music from signs and pictures.

Writing down music in shapes

Try drawing shapes to show how the tune "Twinkle Twinkle Little Star" begins. You need to think carefully about the size, colour and position of the shapes. Try to make the shapes match the sounds you want to show. You can look at the shapes below for some ideas, but try making up your own too.

You could show how long or short the sounds are by the size of your shapes. "Twinkle Twinkle Little Star" starts with six short sounds, followed by a long one.

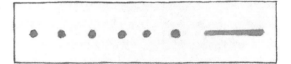

You could draw the shapes getting higher or lower on the page, to show how the tune goes up and down, and where there are jumps between the notes.

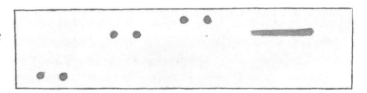

You could use different crayons to show how loudly or quietly to play each sound. You could use bright crayons for loud sounds and pale crayons for quiet sounds.

You could also show which sounds to play on instruments. Think of a different sign for each instrument. You could draw a wavy line for maracas or a star for drums.

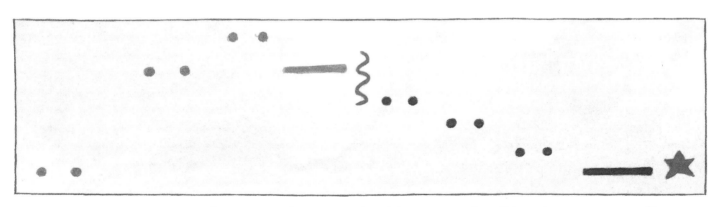

Try writing down another tune in this way. Ask a friend to guess what the tune is. Your friend could think of a tune and write it down too, so you can guess what it is.

You can write down music you make up too. This might help you to remember it, so you can play it again.

Making up new music from shapes

After you have written down a tune in shapes, try turning the page upside down and singing it. You will now have a new tune.

You could also look at it in a mirror to sing it. This will turn it back to front.

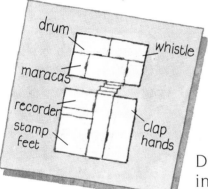

Draw some shapes on a page. Then decide what each one might show and use them to make up some music. Ask a friend to make up some music from your drawing too. It will probably be very different from yours.

If you have written down some of your own music in shapes, you could try asking a friend to play it, without saying what each shape means. Your friend will probably decide on different meanings for your shapes, and make up some new music with them.

Music from pictures

Draw a plan of the rooms in your home and choose a route for walking through them. Choose some sounds for each room. Play the sounds one after another, with walking music in between.

Draw a picture with lots of people in it doing different things, for example, a beach scene or a scene in a park. Decide on sounds for each thing in the picture and then play them as a piece of music.

Writing down music so everyone can read it

Writing down music by drawing or painting shapes can help you to remember tunes and invent new ones.

However, unless you explain all the shapes to other people, they will not know how your music should sound, or how to play it.

Over hundreds of years, people have been inventing a special set of signs for writing down music. Most music is written using these signs, which anyone can learn to read and write. This means they can sing and play music written by other people. You can find out how to read and write some of these signs on pages 40-43.

27

Recording music

You can use a cassette player to record and play back all sorts of sounds, including yourself singing or playing an instrument, and any music you make up. This means you can listen to the sounds more carefully. Recording sounds can also help you to make up new music.

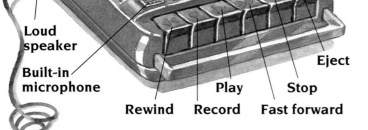

Loud speaker

Built-in microphone

Rewind **Record**

Play

Stop

Fast forward

Eject

Separate microphone

Using a cassette player

Most cassette players work in similar ways. Check the instructions for your machine, or ask an adult to help you.

Many players have a built in microphone, as well as a separate one you can plug in.

Empty spool

At the start of a cassette there is some clear tape. To record, wind forward to the brown tape. You can do this by turning the empty spool with a pencil or finger.

When you make a recording, you destroy what was on the cassette before. You should always check with an adult before you use a cassette, so you do not destroy anything they want to keep.

Experiment to find out how far you need to be from the microphone. If your recording sounds crackly when you play it back, you need to be further from the microphone. If there is a hum in the background, you need to be closer.

Making recordings

Record yourself singing the same tune in a room with soft carpets and curtains, then in one with bare walls and a hard floor. The recordings will sound different. This is because soft surfaces soak up sound, but hard surfaces make it bounce off and echo.

Try recording sounds outside too. You could put a microphone on a window sill overlooking a street and record street sounds. When you play the tape back, see how many different sounds you can hear at once.

To record birdsong, experts use a device called a parabolic reflector to catch the sound. You can try using an umbrella to do this. Point a microphone into the umbrella and tape it to the handle. Point the handle at a place where you often see birds.

Adjust the microphone to find the best position for recording.

Try recording lots of different sounds around the house or outside, such as a tap dripping, an egg frying, a vacuum cleaner and a lawn mower. Play the tape to your friends as a quiz, to see if they can guess what all the different sounds are.

Try recording any pieces of music you make up. This will help you to listen to them more carefully, and means you can keep them to play to other people.

Recording sounds for music

You could make some water music by recording lots of water sounds, such as dripping, pouring, splashing, squirting and bubbling. Try out the sounds first to see which are loud or quiet, long or short. Then decide what order to record them in, and whether to mix different sounds together.

Try mixing recorded sounds with sounds you make with your voice or on an instrument. Start and stop the cassette, adding music in between, or play the music and the tape at the same time. For example you could record sounds at a railway station, then add in your own whistles, running sounds and train rhythms.

Sounds for story music

Here are some tricks for making special sounds for story music. Record them in advance and add them in as you play the music.

Bang two empty yogurt cartons together to make a sound like horses' hooves.

Tap your fingers firmly in a bowl of sugar close to the microphone for a sound like steps on snow.

Run a wet finger around the rim of a glass to make an eerie sound. Do not press too hard or it may break.

Moving to music

Music can often make you want to move around. If you look at people who are listening to music, you often see them tapping their feet or nodding their heads. Moving is a way of joining in with the music you are listening to. You can move your body to show how the music makes you feel.

Showing how music makes you feel

How music makes you feel is called its mood. You can make your body into all sorts of beautiful, weird, fierce or ugly shapes to show the mood of the music.

Listen to some music on a radio, or on a cassette, record or compact disc. Is it fast or slow, jerky or smooth? Think about the mood of the music. Move your whole body into shapes to match the mood.

A gentle, bendy shape

A spiky, twisted shape

A bold, stretchy shape

Now think about moving around the room to the music. How does the music make you want to move? Listen to the speed of the music and fit your movements in with it.

Fast running and jumping movements

Slow turns and bends

Ask a friend to dance while you play some of your own music on a cassette player. Watch how they move to it. Do they move and show the mood as you imagined?

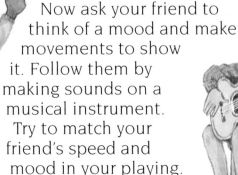

Now ask your friend to think of a mood and make movements to show it. Follow them by making sounds on a musical instrument. Try to match your friend's speed and mood in your playing.

Dances that tell a story

Some dances tell a story by using special steps and movements.

On the right are some movements which ballet dancers use to tell a story.

This means "I am in love".

This means "No!".

This means "I am listening".

Many Indian dances tell stories. The dancers wear bells on their ankles and tap out rhythms with their feet.

Every movement of every part of the dancer's body, head, chin and hands has a special meaning. There are hundreds of hand positions.

This position means "fish".

This position means "A bee hovers over an open lotus flower".

Dancing for fun

Lots of people like dancing with their friends for fun. People invent new dances all the time, and try out new ways to fit steps together.

The waltz is a fairly slow, circling dance which became popular about two hundred years ago.

Jive is the kind of dance that goes with rock and roll music. It became popular in the 1950s. The dancers swing their partners above their heads and between their legs.

Breakdancing was popular in the 1970s and 1980s. It went with a type of music called hip-hop. Some movements are difficult and dangerous.

What musicians do

There are many different kinds of musical jobs. Every concert or recording you hear depends not only on the performers, but on a huge number of other musicians and organizers behind the scenes.

Composing

Composers have to work very hard to make a living. As well as writing music for concerts, many also compose for television or films, and teach other composers. Sometimes musicians ask composers to write music specially for them.

Printing music

Printers make the copies of music sold in shops. They used to do this by scratching the notes back to front on a metal sheet. This was then covered with ink and paper, like a potato in potato printing. Now, most music is produced by computers.

Performing

To be successful, performers have to play or sing brilliantly in every concert. A few become so famous that they can make a career performing alone or with other musicians accompanying.

Many musicians perform in small groups, such as string quartets, deciding together how to play the music. In many larger groups, a person called a conductor tells everyone how to sing or play.

Jazz performers often compose music as they play. This is called improvisation. They also make up new versions of music by other people.

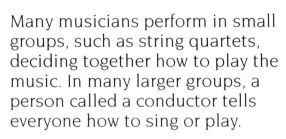

A string quartet
2 violins   1 viola (large violin)   1 cello

Dancing

Dancers have to get to know a piece of music very well to make their steps fit with it. As they dance, they keep listening carefully to make sure all their movements match the speed and mood of the music.

Making recordings

Most recordings are made in special buildings called studios. A record producer works with the musicians to get the best sound.

Often a sound engineer records each voice or instrument separately, then blends them together on a new tape. This is called mixing. The music is often recorded a few times to get the best version possible.

Teaching

Many musicians teach people to sing or play an instrument. They pass on their ways of playing and their ideas about how to interpret music. Some teachers become so famous that people travel across the world to study with them, or to watch them teach in special classes.

Making instruments

Most instruments used by performers have been hand made by instrument makers. It takes many hours of careful work to make each one. Some makers become very famous because their instruments sound so beautiful. Many of these instruments are still played hundreds of years later.

Arranging concerts and shows

Many people work for orchestras and bands, arranging their concerts or shows. They book the halls, organize advertising, arrange the chairs, equipment and music on the day, and organize transport, food and places to stay for the musicians.

Curing musical injuries

Musicians sometimes injure themselves when they play by over-using certain muscles. Doctors help them to relax these muscles so they stop hurting and get stronger.

Music therapy

Music therapists use music to help people who are ill, or cannot move or talk easily. They try to help them become happier and more confident.

33

Why make music?

People make music for all sorts of reasons. All over the world, since the earliest times, music has been used in religious ceremonies, on special occasions, for work and for fun.

Pictures like this were painted about 10,000 years ago on cave walls. They show people clapping.

Many Egyptian paintings show people dancing and playing pipes. They are about 4,000 years old.

Roman paintings are about 2,000 years old. Some show people playing stringed instruments called lyres.

Religion and magic

Many people believe music has magical powers to bring them protection, healing and good luck. Singing and dancing are also important in many different religions, as ways of praying to gods or spirits, and making the services and ceremonies special.

In Thailand, special temple dancers take part in religious ceremonies.

In Peru, some people dance to pray for good weather so that plants will grow.

In Christian churches people sing songs called hymns.

At Chinese New Year, people dance in beautiful dragon costumes, hoping for peace and strength.

Music for work

Old songs known as sea shanties were sung by sailors when hauling up anchors or sails. The regular rhythms helped them to pull together.

Today, many people around the world sing or listen to music while they work. This helps them to concentrate and enjoy their work more.

Background music

Many public places such as train stations, shops and cafés play background music. Often this helps to make customers feel relaxed. Sometimes it drowns out other noises, too.

The music used for films and television has to be carefully chosen or written to help set the mood. For example, loud, fast music might add to the excitement of a car chase.

Advertisements on televison and radio usually have short, catchy tunes. These make you remember the product more easily.

Other reasons for music

Many people listen to music, dance with friends and go to concerts to enjoy themselves. For many people, writing, playing and listening to music is also a serious way of expressing thoughts and feelings, just like painting or writing.

Many countries have their own style of music. Often this has never been written down, but people learn it by listening to it. There is more about music around the world on pages 36-37.

In Europe, music has been written down for hundreds of years. People study the way it has changed during this time to learn more about history. You can find out more about music from the past on pages 38-39.

Music around the world

People in different parts of the world have their own special styles of music. Some of these have hardly changed for hundreds of years. In the past, styles of music were spread from one country to another by people who travelled around. Now, because of recordings, you can hear music from all over the world at home. On these two pages, you can find out about some of the different kinds of music played around the world.

USA

Cajun people live in southwest Louisiana, in the USA. Over many years, they have mixed musical styles together. Today they play violins, accordions, drums and electric guitars.

Russia

Switzerland

Europe

Middle East

Africa

USA

Louisiana

Caribbean

South America

Peru

Bolivia

Caribbean

In parts of the Caribbean, people play drums called pans, which used to be made from empty oil barrels. They play in groups called steel bands.

Africa

In many parts of Africa, people play an instrument made of thin metal strips inside a dried, hollow fruit skin. They pluck the metal strips to make different notes. This also makes pieces of shell attached to the skin buzz.

South America

Musicians in Peru and Bolivia often accompany their songs with bells, drums and panpipes. Panpipes are wooden tubes of different lengths strapped together.

36

Europe

Many European countries have their own special music. In Russia, people play instuments a bit like guitars, called balalaikas. In the Swiss mountains, shepherds play long horns called alphorns.

Japan

In Japan there is a kind of musical play, called noh, which combines music, dance, poetry and costumes. The actors sing the words to drum rhythms. Musicians accompany the dancing by playing flutes and drums, and a stringed instrument called a shamisen.

China

Peking opera, from China, combines acrobatics, pantomime, dance and songs. Musicians play gongs, cymbals, drums, stringed instruments and a kind of mouth organ called a sheng.

Indonesia

A gamelan is a group of instruments from Indonesia. It includes large gongs and instruments similar to glockenspiels. Each musician plays a different version of the same tune.

Australia

Aborigines in Australia make complicated rhythms with sticks and rattles. They also blow and hum into a long hollow instrument called a didjeridu.

Middle East

In many parts of the Middle East, people play a loud reed instrument, similar to an oboe, at open air events such as marches. They puff up their cheeks to blow it.

India

Indian musicians use special rhythm and note patterns to make up new music, using drums called tablas and stringed instruments called sitars.

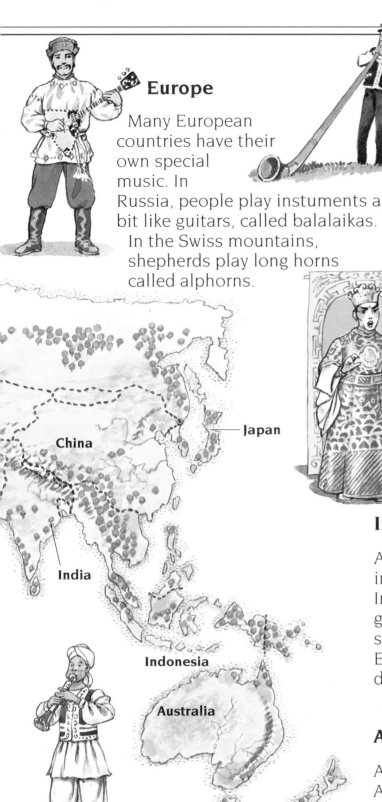

China

Japan

India

Indonesia

Australia

Music from the past

Lots of music written hundreds of years ago is still performed and listened to today. Some old instruments have also survived, as well as paintings and descriptions of them. Studying the ways music and instruments have changed helps us to learn about how people used to live. On these pages you can find out about music in Europe in the past.

Over a thousand years ago in Europe, monks in Christian churches all sang together to the same tune. Little by little this style changed and they began to sing different tunes at the same time. This new style of music was then used by most musicians for hundreds of years.

Hurdy gurdy

Rebec

Music was also a very popular entertainment. Musicians could earn money by singing at village dances and fairs, and at rich people's feasts. They accompanied themselves on instruments such as rebecs and hurdy gurdies. Often they were also jugglers and acrobats.

Virginal

Lute

Recorder

Viol

From about 700 years ago, more ordinary people began to learn to play instruments, such as virginals, lutes, recorders and viols. Music became an important part of education, and people played music with their friends. Music for instruments became as popular as music for voices.

Opera and ballet

About 400 years ago, poets and musicians in Italy began to write musical plays called operas. These soon became very popular.

Many operas used spectacular scenery and special effects. For example, actors might seem to be sitting on clouds above the stage. The clouds were in fact platforms and pulleys, carefully disguised.

Early operas were about heroes in history and legend. Later they were comic stories about ordinary people.

At about the same time, ballet began to develop in France. The first ballet school was soon set up. The basic steps invented there are still used by dancers today.

Orchestras

Orchestras (large groups of instruments) began to be popular more than 300 years ago. Then, they had a harpsichord, stringed instruments and often a few wind instruments in them. As new instruments were invented, they were added to the orchestra. Soon most composers stopped using a harpsichord.

Today, some orchestras have up to 100 players in them. They sometimes include electronic or unusual instruments, which modern composers often use in their music.

Jazz and pop music

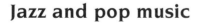

Jazz began nearly 100 years ago in New Orleans in the USA. It was a mixture of many different types of music. Many jazz musicians do not write music down in detail before they play. They start with a tune and then change and decorate it as they go along.

Pop music started to develop about 40 years ago. It mixes together many different styles of music from America, Europe and other countries around the world. Many pop musicians today borrow from past styles, as well as using their own new ideas.

Reading and writing rhythms

On the next four pages you can find out about the most common way to write music down and how to read it. Special signs tell you how long each sound lasts, how high or low it is and how to play or sing it.

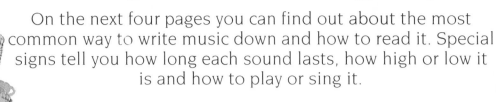

Long and short sounds

Listen to any piece of music. After a while, start to clap along in time with it. Your claps are called beats. The patterns of long and short sounds in the music, called rhythms, fit in around the beats you are clapping.

Words have rhythms too. Imagine a line of washing hung out to dry. Start to clap slow, steady beats, then say the names of the clothes, fitting each name into one beat. Listen to the rhythms you make. Now say the words below, still clapping steadily.

Skirt	T-shirt	Swea-ter	Skirt	Swea-ter	T-shirt	T-shirt	Skirt
CLAP	CLAP	CLAP	CLAP	CLAP	CLAP	CLAP	CLAP

"Skirt" has one long sound. This sound lasts for one beat. "Sweater" and "t-shirt" both have two short sounds. The two short sounds together take up one beat.

When you read music, you can tell how many beats a sound lasts for by its shape. You can see what the rhythm you are saying looks like below.

Skirt   T - shirt Swea - ter Skirt   Swea - ter T - shirt T - shirt Skirt

This sign shows that the sound lasts for one beat. It is called a crotchet, or quarter note.

This sign shows two sounds which last half a beat each. They are quavers, or eighth notes.

A quaver, or eighth note, on its own

Putting sounds in groups

In most music the beats are put in groups called bars. The bars are separated by lines called bar lines. Two numbers called the time signature tell you how to count.

The top number tells you how many beats are in a bar. The bottom one shows what each beat is. 4 means crotchet (quarter note) beats.

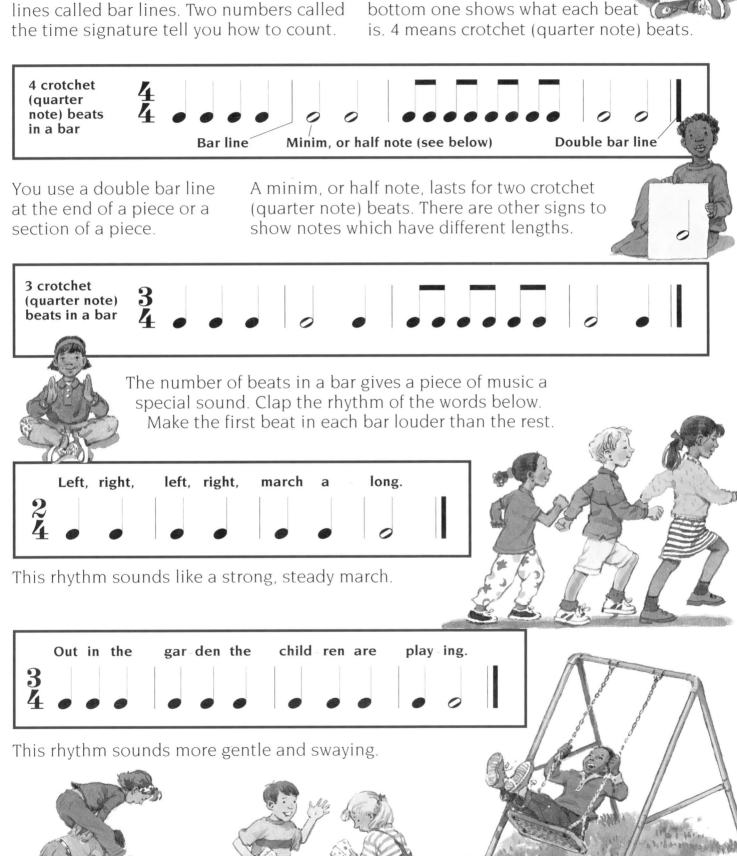

4 crotchet (quarter note) beats in a bar

Bar line   Minim, or half note (see below)   Double bar line

You use a double bar line at the end of a piece or a section of a piece.

A minim, or half note, lasts for two crotchet (quarter note) beats. There are other signs to show notes which have different lengths.

3 crotchet (quarter note) beats in a bar

The number of beats in a bar gives a piece of music a special sound. Clap the rhythm of the words below. Make the first beat in each bar louder than the rest.

Left, right,   left, right,   march a   long.

This rhythm sounds like a strong, steady march.

Out in the   gar-den the   child-ren are   play-ing.

This rhythm sounds more gentle and swaying.

Reading and writing tunes

The exact highness or lowness of a sound is called its pitch. You can show the rough shape of a tune by putting signs higher or lower on a page. However, to show the exact pitch of notes, you have to put them on, or between, lines.

Find three similar bottles and pour different amounts of water in them. Blow over the three bottles, the one with least water in first and the one with most water in last, to make a pattern of notes which goes low, middle, high. You can show this pattern of sounds by putting three signs getting higher up the page.

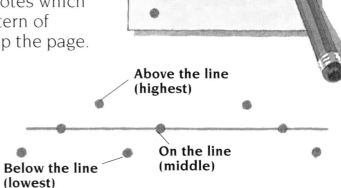

Above the line (highest)

On the line (middle)

Below the line (lowest)

If you draw a line straight through the signs for the middle note, you make it easier in a long tune to see exactly which bottle to blow next. A note below a line is lower than a note on the line, which is lower than a note above the line.

You can also play this pattern on a keyboard by playing a note on your left (low), a note in the middle and a note on your right (high).

Using five lines

Most music is written on a set of five lines, called a staff or stave. The notes fit on the lines and in the spaces between. You draw short lines above or below the staff for higher or lower notes.

Look at the pattern of notes going up and down a staff, and imagine the notes linked in a wavy line. This will help you to see the shape of a tune. Then you can use the lines and spaces of the staff to calculate exactly which notes are in the tune. (You can see how to do this on the next page.)

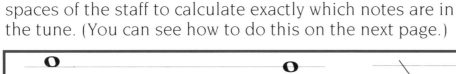

Where the notes go on a staff

Each musical pitch has a name. Pitches are named after the first seven letters of the alphabet. As the pitches get higher, their names go from A to G then start at A again. You put a sign called a clef at the start of a staff to show which pitch is on each line.

On the right is a treble clef. It curls around the next to bottom line of a staff. You use it to show that a note on this line is G. This means the space above this line is A, the next line is B, and so on.

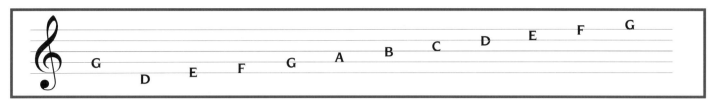

Finding the notes on a keyboard

On a keyboard, the keys are named after the pitches they play. Look carefully at the black keys. Can you see that they are arranged in a pattern which repeats all along the keyboard? All the keys with the same letter name are in the same place in the pattern. You can see the names of the keys in the picture below.

Find a white key just left of two black keys. This is C. Play all the other Cs too. They are higher and lower versions of the same note. The C nearest the middle of the keyboard is Middle C.

2 black keys   **3 black keys**   **2 black keys**   **3 black keys**

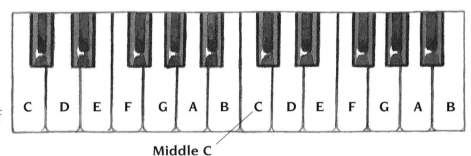

Middle C

Put your right hand thumb on Middle C, and rest your fingers on the next four white keys. Press these keys one after the other from left to right, starting with your thumb. The staff on the right shows you which notes you are playing. (The treble clef shows you where the G above Middle C is on the staff.)

C D E F G

To write music down you combine rhythm signs (see pages 40-41) with pitch signs on a staff. This means you know how high or low each note is and how long it lasts. You also use other words and signs which tell you things like how loud or quiet, fast or slow, spiky or smooth the music is.

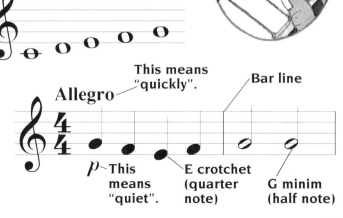

This means "quickly".

Bar line

Allegro

p This means "quiet".

E crotchet (quarter note)

G minim (half note)

Learning an instrument

If you enjoy listening to music, you might like to learn to play an instrument. Playing music can be great fun, though to play well you have to work hard too. These two pages are about how to choose an instrument to learn.

Think about the kind of music you want to play and the instruments you like to listen to. Some instruments are mainly used in pop groups or orchestras. Some can be used in many different kinds of music.

Do you want to play alone or in a group? Most music is for more than one player, but there is lots of music to play alone on the piano or guitar.

Some instruments may suit you better than others. To play some you need long arms or legs, or strong teeth. Ask to try out some instruments in a music shop to see which are comfortable to hold and play.

You can often rent an instrument from a music shop. This means you can try it out at home to see whether you like it. Also, find out if your school can lend you one.

If there are no instrumental teachers at your school, you can try to find a teacher by asking at a music shop or library, or by looking in a local paper or directory.

Stringed instruments

Stringed instruments come in small sizes for young people to play.

The violin has lots of music written for it, and is a good instrument to learn if you want to play in an orchestra. At first, it can be hard to make a nice sound.

The cello is also a good choice if you want to play in an orchestra. It is easier to play at first than a violin, but you need fairly long legs to hold it properly.

The electric guitar is a good instrument to learn if you want to play pop music. For the classical guitar, there are many other kinds of music to play, either on your own or in a group.

Wind instruments

The wind instruments below are all good to start on. Do not play for too long at first though, because blowing them uses up lots of breath and can make you feel a bit dizzy.

Recorders are simple to learn and they are good for playing with friends. They are also very cheap to buy.

The flute is fairly easy to learn. To play it, your arms need to be long enough to hold it level. It is also easier to blow if you do not have big front teeth.

The clarinet is used in both orchestras and bands. You need to have strong front teeth to blow it. Make sure your fingers are big enough to reach all the keys and cover the holes.

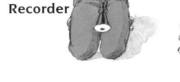

Cornet

Recorder

Trumpet

Flute

Clarinet

The cornet is a good choice if you would like to play in a brass band. Trumpets are used in more kinds of music, but you should not play one unless you have strong teeth.

Tenor horn

The tenor horn is easier to blow than the cornet or trumpet. It is also easier to hold. It is mainly used in brass band music.

Tablas

Other instruments

Drums are used in most kinds of music. To play them you need to be very good at making rhythms. You can start to learn on a snare drum, Indian tablas, African bongos or, if you can reach all the drums, a full drum kit.

There is lots of music written for the piano, both to play alone and with other people. Learning it can also help you to read music well, because you have to play several notes together.

Electronic keyboards are good for playing lots of music. Most can make lots of different sounds and rhythms, and record your playing. You can usually use headphones too, so that you do not disturb other people.

Listening to music

The more carefully you listen to music, the more you will enjoy it. Try these listening exercises with everyday sounds, to help you listen more closely when you hear, play or make up music.

A listening walk

Next time you go for a walk near where you live, stop from time to time to listen. Make a list of all the different sounds you can hear around you. How many sounds can you hear at a time?

Try this when you go to other places, for example a busy town, a field, a railway station or the seaside. Are there some sounds you can hear in all these places?

Voices and soundtracks

Listen carefully to people as they talk, and think about what makes each voice sound different. Are they high or low, loud or quiet, gentle or gruff, jerky or smooth? What other words describe them?

When you are watching the television or a film, listen carefully to the music soundtrack. Try to decide what it is about the music which helps to set the mood. For example, a jerky rhythm might make you laugh, a slow tune might make you feel sad, and sounds that suddenly get louder and end in a crash might make you frightened.

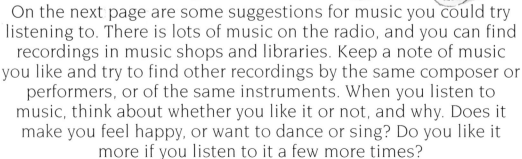

On the next page are some suggestions for music you could try listening to. There is lots of music on the radio, and you can find recordings in music shops and libraries. Keep a note of music you like and try to find other recordings by the same composer or performers, or of the same instruments. When you listen to music, think about whether you like it or not, and why. Does it make you feel happy, or want to dance or sing? Do you like it more if you listen to it a few more times?

Piano, organ and harpsichord
Beethoven: Moonlight Sonata (piano)
Schubert: Moments Musicaux (piano)
Chopin: Waltzes (piano)
Scott Joplin: The Entertainer (piano)
Debussy: Children's Corner (piano)
Art Tatum: Piano Discoveries (jazz piano)
Bach: Toccata and Fugue in D minor (organ)
Widor: Toccata from Organ Symphony no.5
Couperin: Harpsichord music
Bach: Italian Concerto (harpsichord)

Wind instruments
Handel: Fitzwilliam Sonatas (recorder)
Vivaldi: Flute Concerto
Vaughan Williams: Oboe Concerto
Mozart: Clarinet Concerto
Haydn: Trumpet Concerto
Mozart: Serenade for 13 instruments
Charlie Parker: Scrapple from the Apple
    (jazz saxophone)
Miles Davis: Tutu (jazz trumpet)

Stringed instruments
Vivaldi: The Four Seasons (violin)
Mendelssohn: Violin Concerto
Haydn: Cello Concerto no.1
Elgar: Cello Concerto
Rodrigo: Concierto de Aranjuez (guitar)
Tchaikovsky: Serenade for Strings
Dvořák: American Quartet

Electric and electronic instruments
Jimi Hendrix: All Along the Watchtower
    (electric guitar)
Michael Jackson: Human Nature
    (electronic keyboards)

Orchestra music
Mozart: Symphony no.40
Beethoven: Pastoral Symphony
Mendelssohn: Fingal's Cave
Tchaikovsky: 1812 Overture
Sibelius: Finlandia
Holst: The Planets

Bartók: Concerto for Orchestra
Britten: The Young Person's Guide to
    the Orchestra

Songs
Elizabethan madrigals
Elgar: Sea Pictures
Canteloube: Songs of the Auvergne
Nina Simone: My baby just cares for me
Beach Boys: Little Deuce Coupe
Beatles: In my life
Wham: Wake me up before you go-go
Bobby McFerrin: Take the 'A' Train (scat
    singing, see page 18)
Prince: Diamonds and Pearls

Choir music, operas and musicals
Tallis: If ye love me
Purcell: Rejoice in the Lord alway
Mozart: Ave verum corpus
Brahms: How lovely are thy dwellings fair
Purcell: Dido and Aeneas
Mozart: The Magic Flute
Humperdinck: Hansel and Gretel
Britten: The Little Sweep
Lerner and Loewe: My Fair Lady
Bernstein: West Side Story
Rodgers and Hammerstein: The Sound
    of Music

Ballet music
Delibes: Coppélia
Tchaikovsky: The Nutcracker
Stravinsky: Petrushka
Ravel: Daphnis and Chloé
Prokofiev: Romeo and Juliet

Musical shapes, ideas and stories
Ravel: Bolero (ostinato drum rhythms, see
    page 22)
Smetana: Vltava (describes a river)
Saint-Saëns: Carnival of the Animals
Dukas: The Sorcerer's Apprentice (story of
    a magic spell gone wrong)
Debussy: La Mer (describes the sea)

Index

First published in 1993 by Usborne Publishing Ltd, 83-85 Saffron Hill, London EC1N 8RT, England. Copyright © 1993 Usborne Publishing Ltd. The name Usborne and the device 🎈 are Trade Marks of Usborne Publishing Ltd. All rights reserved. No part of this publication may be reproduced, stored in a retrieval system or transmitted in any form or by any means, electronic, mechanical, photocopying, recording or otherwise, without the prior permission of the publisher. UE.
Printed in Spain.
First published in America March 1994.